Widowspeak

by Renee J. Wurzer

a Renew Collaborative project

St Louis MO   Eau Claire WI

with special thanks to Fred A. Brede, Brede Publishing

Widowspeak

Copyright ©2016, 2017, 2018 by Renee J. Wurzer

All rights reserved. No part of this publication may be reproduced, stored in a retrieval system, or transmitted in any form or by any means—electronic, mechanical, photocopy, recording, or any other—except for brief quotations in printed reviews, without the prior permission of the author.

Unless otherwise indicated, all Scripture taken from the Holy Bible, NEW INTERNATIONAL VERSION®, NIV® Copyright © 1973, 1978, 1984, 2011 by Biblica, Inc.® Used by permission. All rights reserved worldwide.

Design: Fred A. Brede, Brede Publishing
Cover photo: Snow Trottier-Polmanter
Author photo: Kathryn Victoria Photography

Printed in the United States of America

ISBN: 9781731280749

dedicated to

the widowed
Ellen, Hertha, Kay, Judy
Hilda, Betty
Bertha, Beatrice, Jeanne
Janet, Betty
Brandi, Maggie, Nancy
Kathie, Jacki, Jackie, Cathy
Jerry, Joseph

and

the orphaned
Amy, Bryan
Brandon

with immense gratitude for my *first five*

Amy
Bryan
Tami
Perry
Andrea

and all those who walk with me
on this earthly journey

contents

1 **Departure** 1
2 **Widowspeak** 15
3 **Words** 21
4 **Password** 29
5 **Laughter** 33
6 **Obituary** 37
7 **Unbalanced** 43
8 **Day 23** 49
9 **Lists** 53
10 **Sex** 61
11 **Love** 71
12 **23 Again** 75
13 **Performance Theater** 83
14 **Surrender** 85
Resources

Widowspeak

a story of grief and joy

Chapter 1 Widowspeak

1

Departure

There is a moment when you realize you are being *cared for, protected*. For me, that moment was shortly after the police sergeant came out the door of the back porch, the porch that leads to our kitchen, the door we use every day. Behind him is someone new. The sergeant makes the introductions. The man is from the cremation society, the one called a short while ago, the one called because of the privacy and respect given to the family of a recently-deceased friend. The man offers his condolences. He's the eighth man, the seventh stranger, to do so this morning. The EMTs, the fire department station captain, the police sergeant and the coroner—each of these men offered his condolences in the living room, before I moved to the back yard, before this moment, the moment I realize *I am being protected*.

The reason I am sitting in the back yard is my husband. He died this morning, cardiac arrest, a decade earlier than we'd expected or planned. The man from the cremation society is here to assist. He is here to assist me, the widow. He is here to assist the family of the deceased and the emergency personnel. He is here to assist in removing the body from the basement, the body, my husband. No one wanted me to watch that process. No one wanted me to see that happen. That is why I am in the back yard, in this lawn chair, a place where I cannot watch or see.

Earlier this morning, after the coroner had departed and before this man arrived, I had returned to the basement.

in the stillness of time
between the departure of the EMTs
and the arrival of the funeral director
I remove the shoes from my husband's feet
and lie down beside him
resting my head on his shoulder
cherishing time

The coroner had gone to the basement earlier, made his analysis, and cleaned up the medical intervention sites with a washcloth. Before he'd gone to the basement, he included me in the care of my husband by asking me for the washcloth. In the basement he'd gathered up the discarded medical supplies, the pullover hoodie and t-shirt that the EMTs had cut off, a lighter and pack of cigarettes.

I remember the coroner being near the front door, his back to the wall, knees bent, achieving a height matching my seated position, casually and intentionally positioning himself so that we are able to comfortably converse. He shares with me his findings—cardiac arrest—asking if I need an autopsy. Without hesitation I reply: *No. I don't. Do you?*

He does not.

I close my eyes, teary with emotion and thankful there will be no autopsy. The tension within me is released, a slow jagged exhalation of breath.

My mind and body remember the panic that set in earlier when the police sergeant told me the next step was to call the coroner. My heart had skipped a beat. I'd heard stories, terrible stories of families in an adjoining county waiting hours for the coroner to arrive. Panic evident in my body and on my face, I stammer: *How long? How long will he take to get here?*

I receive the response: *Usually 15 to 20 minutes.* Anxiety dissipates. Comfort fills my soul.

The coroner has now departed. Our daughter goes downstairs; this is her time with Dad. She is aware that to be present in this moment is a blessing. She takes a series of photographs with her cell phone in the event her brother, who is hours away, will need or want to see the images.

When she comes upstairs I leave the wicker rocker and make my way down the stairs. I bring a rug with me, a clean soft faded cotton rug. I lay the rug next to my husband then turn and remove his shoes before lying down beside him, resting my head on his shoulder. Harley, our dog, has come with me. He sniffs around, seems to understand that death has visited, then wanders off to explore. I don't know how long I lay there, next to my husband, eyes closed, remembering, my head nestled next to his, taking in the shape of his shoulder, absorbing the sensation, finding comfort, cherishing time, knowing this would be the last time we'd touch.

Time passes. I hear new and unfamiliar footsteps on the living room floor above me. I hear our daughter's voice. She comes down the stairway.

I get up, turn away from my husband and walk across the basement, climbing the stairs behind her. I do not look back. Our daughter will later share with me that I'd been in the basement 30 minutes.

Did I carry the dog upstairs? I do not remember. When I reach the top of the stairs, I am ushered through the kitchen and out the back porch door.

A few minutes later, in the back yard just outside the door, the man from the cremation society stands in front of me. I am sitting in a plastic lawn chair, sensing no need to stand as business etiquette and common courtesy might dictate. His body language tells me it is not necessary.

He selects and confirms an appointment for me to meet with him tomorrow morning, Friday at 10:30 at the cremation society. His manner is gentle. He speaks softly and clearly, in simple sentences. *Do I know the location?*

Yes.

Handing me his business card, he equips me with the address and phone number. In this basic yet complex exchange he gives me permission to fully and simply BE—to be early, to be on time, to be late—a gesture of compassion and understanding. He knows the difficulties ahead, realities not yet familiar to me.

I promise to call if we are going to be late. My response includes more than just me. Our daughter is sitting next to me. Now, as I write I wonder, was her fiancé there too? He'd been there earlier, when we were in the living room. I don't remember if he is with us in this moment, in the back yard.

Our daughter, her fiancé, our son and his wife, the grandchildren, officially transition. In the wake of death we are now tenderly and in hushed tones referred to as *the family*. I am *the widow*. I receive the business card. There is comfort in accepting care.

My husband is no longer on the basement floor. He is—or rather his body is—in the back of a hearse, or an ambulance, or whatever vehicle is used for that purpose. I didn't think about it until I began to write this, and now uncovering which vehicle transported him doesn't offer enough solace for me to expend the energy. Whatever vehicles the men arrived in—and the one my husband departed in—are now gone.

...

Pause to remember a time when you were comforted by giving over the role of caregiver and quietly accepting care.

...

Time passes. Time stands still. I am sitting in a lawn chair in the back yard. The grass is lush and green. The day is warm. The sky was sunny this morning and is now overcast. I sit in the chair, barefoot, wearing two dresses and tear stains. There is quiet all around me. My heart feels protected and a bit distant, as though someone has nestled it within a huge basket of cotton, then tucked the basket away where my mind will not disturb it, a place where sounds are soft and muffled, a place of peace. My heart is in the expansive and gentle hands of God. My heart is held by *YAHWEH*, my Creator and my Lord.

Our daughter is here, her fiancé nearby. Our son, daughter-in-law and two grandkids are on their way from a distant city, choosing to drive after checking airline schedules for last-minute flights. The four of them will arrive later tonight. The journey will take eight to ten hours depending on toddler necessitated play and potty breaks.

Time stretches out before me—48 hours—the waiting time required by law between death and cremation. My husband wanted to be cremated. He wanted cremation and a beer party. He wanted us to gather together, to tell stories, to laugh and remember him.

...

*Pause to remember a time when
God protected your heart.*

...

It is Thursday and it is morning and my husband is dead. This unexpected undertaking began when I arrived home from work a few hours ago, just after 9:30am. I called out a greeting, probably *Honey, I'm home,* and did not find it odd that there was no response.

We're married. We've lived, loved, argued, cohabitated, co-parented and co-labored for more than 30 years. He might be listening to music on his MP3; he might have walked over to the local food store; he might be ignoring me. Marriage deafness, it happens.

Unaware of all that is about to transpire, I change out of my red polo and khakis into a short black cotton-casual summer dress—cool, comfortable, well-worn, washed many times. As I come from the bedroom into the kitchen I notice he's carried up the flowering-plant food I'd asked about yesterday and a few summer things we'd stored in the basement over winter.

There's a fresh pot of coffee.

That he'd remembered to bring up the plant food and make a fresh pot of coffee were signs that he was listening, tangible indicators of his love.

...

Reflection:
How do you receive love?
How do you show love?

...

Something though is not quite right. His bike and his Jeep are both here. If he'd walked to the local food store he'd be back by now. The basement light is on and the door is open, so I'm curious and a little bit perturbed at being ignored, I call out, Hey, babe, I'm home? as I start down the stairs.

At step nine—there are thirteen—I can see his black sweat-pants and white athletic shoes. He is lying on the floor near the far wall, in front of the workbench. In one breath I am across the basement.

He is lying on his back. His right leg is elevated, bent at the knee. I grab his knee and shake it as though to wake him from sleeping. He is unconscious, eyelids slightly open. His rimless glasses are askew, crooked from the impact of falling. His skin is a darker-than-normal shade of red. I do not feel death, yet I know something is terribly wrong. I call his name. I call his name again perhaps even a third, fourth, or fifth time before running up the stairs to find my phone.

Standing in the front entrance of the apartment where the cell reception is best, I dial 9-1-1. The dispatcher answers. I hold my breath and respond to her questions with data. She is sending an ambulance. Help is on the way.

Then, something unexpected: the dispatcher asks if I am with my husband.

I am not.

He's in the basement.

I am upstairs.

I taste guilt and shame, caught in the wrong place at the wrong time.

You know better than this! Shame on you, silently screams a familiar and ruthless voice.[1]

...

Pause to remember a time you experienced guilt or shame. Explore the validity of these sensations.

...

The dispatcher directs me to go to my husband, to go downstairs. She is calm. She is supportive. She is not the voice of shame. I move quickly, thankful the apartment is small and manageable and he is nearby. I let her know when I reach him.

She replies with the announcement that we're going to do chest compressions. She will count. I will compress. Put one hand here, the other on top of it there. Now 1-2-3-4, 1-2-3-4, 1-2-3-4 …

My body obeys her count. My mind and heart wander decades at the speed of thought. I am doing CPR chest compressions. I know how to do CPR. I've known how to do CPR for the past 41 years, since my first summer in Red Cross Senior Life Saving classes, on the beach at the state park when I was just 13 years old; then again

---

[1] Guilt is *I did something*, Shame is *I am something* – Andrea M. Polnaszek, LCSW, author of *The Elijah Project*, identifying our feelings and learning to express our emotions in a God honoring way, andreapolnaszek.com.

when I worked at a manufacturing company, and again when I worked at the hospital. All those years of knowing and never using, never needing, all those years were for today.

I hear his bones cracking, giving way to this violent act, a brutal hope that life is within this body—a gruesome thought, an unsettling affirmation. The compression needs to be great enough to move the heart. 1-2-3-4, 1-2-3-4, 1-2-3-4 … my cell phone—a black flip phone—drops from its unstable location between my right shoulder and my ear. I yell to the dispatcher my own counts 1-2-3-4, 1-2-3-4, 1-2-3-4 … there is a distracting counter-motion, something in the pocket of the pullover hoodie he's wearing: a drill bit, a lighter, his cigarettes.

As the rhythm of pauses and compressions permits, I toss these unruly items next to the cell phone that landed on the floor just past his left shoulder.

Something deep within me emerges: a primal and instinctive impulse, a memory, a dream, a deep knowing that someday this life-and-death struggle would happen, that this was in our destiny but not our destination—that this was happening way too soon, that this was happening in God's perfect timing.

Sometime just after the cigarettes come to rest on the floor near his shoulder I experience a brief burst of anger. Tears form at the corners of my eyes. I am angry about the cigarettes and feeling cheated. Forgetting God's sovereignty over life and death, I yell at my husband. He does not respond.

I am suddenly and violently aware of an insidious enticement to helplessness—a dark and dangerous state devoid of hope—lurking in the shadowed corners of the basement. Just outside the circle of incandescent light, evil is ready and waiting to destroy me.

...
*Pause to remember a time when you
encountered hopelessness.
Reflection:
How were you challenged?
How were you changed?*
...

The repetitive motion of the compressions sears my out-of-practice muscles. 1-2-3-4, 1-2-3-4, 1-2-3-4, 1-2-3-4, 1-2-3-4, 1-2 … I grow weary. I must keep going.

Then a sound reaches me. I hear the sirens, faint at first, growing stronger. Relief floods my whole being and the evil of hopelessness retreats, returning to hide in the darkness. The first responders come down the stairs, take over the care of my husband.

One tells me to go upstairs. I want to stay. I want to help move the clutter out of the way, to make room. He tells me a second time to go upstairs. This time I obey.

Time passes. Time stands still. I am in the lawn chair in the back yard. Time—48 hours—stretches out before me.

I begin to remember other deaths, funerals of loved ones, my husband's wishes, the way he sensed my discomfort, looked into my eyes then held my hand just before the funeral mass for his mother.

My heart needs a quiet space in the stillness of time. He is not here to hold my hand.

We were private people, preferring the company of each other and our children much, much more than extended family, impulsive visitors, or even close friends in times of crisis, life-and-death struggle. In the aftermath of the chaos in all that just happened, there is stillness. As I relax into our tradition of privacy my mind begins to look forward. My heart yearns to move as slowly and deliberately as possible. All that needs to begin will wait until our son and his family arrive. Then we will let others know. My husband has eight siblings; his mother and father have passed away. My parents are living and my two sisters also need to know. His siblings first, then mine. This task, calling the siblings, can wait until after I reach our friend and pastor. He is on sabbatical; he and his family are on vacation.

I will wait until evening to make the call disrupting their time away with news of unexpected death. I never imagined making such a call. I am undone at the prospect of sharing the news of my husband's death.

This morning when the sirens stopped and the emergency personnel first arrived, there was a barrage of questions for me: husband's full name, date of birth, social security number, medications and medical history. In the moment I give the wrong birth year, realize it, then perfectly recall the social security number. My husband's wallet is a few feet away; I right the wrong by retrieving his driver's license.

When we finish the Q&A, the police sergeant asks if there is anyone I need to call. Five people come to mind: daughter, son, friend, pastor, friend. The call to our daughter is first. I ask her to head to the hospital, to call her brother, to call our friend asking for prayer. Then, I walk into the master bedroom, kneel

> I walk into the master bedroom, kneel down on my husband's side of the bed and pray, daring to hope, praying for the miracle, the Lazarus death-to-life miracle.

down on my husband's side of the bed and pray, daring to hope, praying for the miracle, the Lazarus death-to-life miracle.[2]

...

Pause to remember a time when you kneeled to pray.
Reflection:
How did God answer your prayer?

...

Believing wholeheartedly that miracle and medical often coincide, I prepare to go with the ambulance when it departs for the hospital, to join our daughter and stay there bed-side with my husband.

While the EMTs work, I pack my husband's medications and other items he'll need. Looking down at my clothing, I realize for the first time that in an apartment filled with men I am nearly naked in my short black cotton-casual summer dress.

I walk quickly to my closet and pull a shapeless khaki jumper—a tent-like garment—over the top of what I am already wearing. Good enough.

...

Pause to remember a time when your personal appearance didn't matter, when whatever you were wearing was good enough.
Reflection:
Did this experience change you? How so?

...

---

[2] The biblical story of Jesus raising Lazarus from the dead is in John 11:1-44.

Time passes. Time stops.

In the living room the sergeant comes toward me, quietly. He offers his condolences; the team had been in direct contact with the doctor, all medical options had been exhausted, my husband had not responded, he is dead.

Did the sergeant lead me to the rocker in the corner by the bookcase, where I could see the empty gurney waiting on the front sidewalk just outside the door? I don't remember how I got to the chair—my familiar wicker rocker—pushed aside to make a path for the gurney we never used.

I call our daughter; tell her to come to the apartment instead of the hospital.

I am sitting in the rocker when the emergency personnel working to save my husband come up from the basement and walk through the living room, each stopping to look me in the eyes and offer me his condolences.

>Agony.
>
>Shallow breathing.
>
>Silent tears.

If my life story were a movie, the soundtrack for this moment would be bagpipes. Distant. Foreign. Ancient. Eerie. The faint melody, *Amazing Grace*. On screen an actress-as-me would be sitting in a rocker silently grieving as a thick fog rolls down the street and across the lawn, and the camera fades to black.

So David arose from the ground, washed, anointed himself, and changed his clothes; and he came into the house of the LORD and worshiped. Then he came to his own house, and when he requested, they set food before him and he ate.

[21] Then his servants said to him, "What is this thing that you have done? While the child was alive, you fasted and wept; but when the child died, you arose and ate food."

[22] He said, "While the child was still alive, I fasted and wept; for I said, 'Who knows, the LORD may be gracious to me, that the child may live.' [23] "But now he has died; why should I fast? Can I bring him back again? I will go to him, but he will not return to me." – 2 Samuel 12:20-23 NASB

The thief comes only to steal and kill and destroy; I [Jesus] came that they may have life, and have it abundantly. – John 10:10 NASB

The LORD your God is in your midst,
The Mighty One, will save;
He will rejoice over you with gladness,
He will quiet you with His love,
He will rejoice over you with singing.
       – Zephaniah 3:17 NKJV

2

Widowspeak

I am a speaker and writer of words—and when my husband died grief hit me hard. Missing him so fully that I engage in thoughts of suicide—I find it difficult to breathe, difficult to do the most of basic of tasks. I experience a startling and frustrating reduction in my cognitive ability, the emotional trauma displacing about 20% of my vocabulary. In conversation after conversation I search for words, interjecting long pauses as I wait and wait and wait for my brain to retrieve what I need. Often the words elude me for extended periods of time, hide from me for days, only to reappear randomly while I am doing the dishes or mowing the lawn, the person I'd been conversing with having long returned to her or his own life.

I am a woman seeking to inspire others with courage and hope in Christ—and the first chapter of my book, this book, tells the story in the jumbled sequence of my widowhood. It is my *widowspeak*, the honest-as-possible retelling, the difficult-to-follow paragraphs bearing witness to the unimaginable trauma of deep grief.

I am a flawed, human and fragile encourager—and I am a woman whose confidence is reduced to rubble, a woman who lost her closest ally and confidant, a woman vulnerable and exposed and desperately in need of unconditional love, grace, compassion and encouragement.[3]

---

[3] *I am ... a flawed, human and fragile encourager* is from my blog, the self-descriptive words I first embraced in 2009.

...

Pause to remember times in your life when you received unconditional love, grace, compassion, or encouragement.

...

In this unlikely state, I set off to write a book. That sentence brings to mind *Don Quixote*. Am I tilting at windmills? Imagining giants? Affirming *Dulcinea*? [4]

My hope is to dislodge the complacency within other relationships, other marriages—that you will begin to live life to the fullest. My husband and I thought we had more time, years of more time. Why do we refuse to face our endings, the reality that death will part us, that today may be our day?

> My hope is to dislodge the complacency within other relationships, other marriages—that you will begin to live life to the fullest.

In the years when the kids were young we purchased life insurance, wrote wills, selected guardians. Once the kids grew to be adults we faced a few medical challenges and set aside time for celebrating life, listening to music, seeing movies, imagining the *what if* of winning the lottery, dreaming about places our hearts longed to travel, enjoying our precious children and grandchildren, making known our wishes for cremation, living our faith in Christ and resurrection—our hope in God's promise of life after death.

My husband and I had talked about his death coming before mine, ending our marriage, our friendship, life as we knew it. Looking at our family histories we could see it was likely I'd outlive him. We spoke of the things I'd do, my passions, my ministry, my

---

[4] *The Ingenious Nobleman Sir Quixote of La Mancha* is a Spanish novel by Miguel de Cervantes Saavedra. See also, the movie *Man of La Mancha* (1972) starring Peter O'Toole, Sophia Loren and James Coco.

hope. Yet, the opposite was also possible, that I'd die first, so we talked of what he would do in the years ahead without me.

Strangely these discussions were not gruesome or morbid; we discovered comfort in knowing life will be celebrated, that the people we love most will live on. I wrote the blog *Heartbeat* in 2011, years before my husband's death.

Blog: Heartbeat

If it were 15 minutes before the world ends—and I am given the grace to know—what will I say? I will speak of grace. God's grace. I will spend these last minutes holding the hand and the heart of my husband. I will think of our children and the people our children love, I will celebrate my sisters and my friends, my nieces and nephews, and the deep connections I have made along the way with my children of the heart.

In the final 15 minutes that my heart beats, I reach out and take your hand. You are so very special. You are as God intended you to be, your gifts and joys, the life of grace laid out before you were a heartbeat in your mother's womb. Every breath drawn on this earth is a gift. Each smile a glimpse of heaven.

I ask you to stop and celebrate, to look back on the joy in your life, to re-encounter the moments when life felt so very right, the moments when every piece of the puzzle that is you fell into place and you were alive with every fiber in your being. Heart. Mind. Soul. Heart, Mind, Soul in Communion with God. Not the sterile churchy communion, but true Community. Heart on fire. Mind humming with possible impossibilities. Soul feeling so deeply that the passion comes alive.

> I will speak of grace. God's grace, waiting for us, not just here on earth but in the next life. I believe that yes, we can take it with us—this life, our family and friends, the people we love.
>
> Christ died because He loves us. Reach for the grace. Today. Tomorrow. Forever.

Heartbeat was inspired by the *15 Minutes to Live* writing assignment prepared by Gwen Bell: You just discovered you have 15 minutes to live. Set a timer for 15 minutes. Write the story that has to be written.[5]

> *"We are afraid of truth, afraid of fortune, afraid of death, and afraid of each other. Our age yields no great and perfect persons."*
> – Ralph Waldo Emerson

What my husband and I could not even begin to understand is the depth of the pain, the feeling of amputation, the undeniable deep truth that I do not want to go on living if living means being without him.

> *In my Father's house are many rooms. If it were not so, would I have told you that I go to prepare a place for you?* [3] *And if I go and prepare a place for you, I will come again and will take you to myself, that where I am you may be also.* [4] *And you know the way to where I am going.* – John 14:2-4 ESV

---

[5] *Heartbeat* was written as an assignment from the Trust Yourself (#Trust30) Writing Challenge an online initiative of Seth Godin and The Domino Project, including quotes from Ralph Waldo Emerson.

. . .

Reflection:
Set a timer for 15 minutes. Write the words that need to be written.

. . .

DAY 14

JOURNAL: Today, my love, I awoke with the most comforting sensation, expecting you to be on your side of our bed. I am not even in our bed, but resting in the guestroom, yet you are here.

I want to stay in this moment, hold gently the fragile serenity of waking together, the intimacy layered and woven by years of sleeping next to this one man, to languish in the dream of life rather than face the sharp reality of living what has become a nightmare. Satan is maximizing every opportunity. Anxiety is too familiar. Thoughts of suicide assault me daily. In the wake of the fragile serenity of this morning, the guided journaling of my grief reveals something stunning: my husband, the man I lost, is the person best suited to comfort me.

. . .

Reflection:
Who do you turn to for comfort?
Who are you best suited to comfort?

. . .

DAY 113

JOURNAL: Today I stopped by Altered Ego, the art studio and salon, and our dear friend—like a hummingbird—attends to all that is happening in her place of ministry, in her place of business, and I feel loved. Surrounded by canvas artwork, old doors repurposed, refinished wood furniture and hand-made jewelry, I sip my mug of coffee. I am intrigued by I AM FREE painted mocha hands on a soft blue canvas, real ropes around the wrists—once binding, now cut— the hands free to move. We talk about scars and Christ and heaven.

> "Where you used to be, there is a hole in the world, which
> I find myself constantly walking around in the daytime,
> and falling in at night. I miss you like hell."
> – Edna St. Vincent Millay [6]

---

[6] Source: *A Widow's Guide to Healing: Gentle Support and Advice for the First 5 Years* by Kristin Meekhof, LMSW and James Windell, MA.

3
Words

Since 2009 I've been writing and publishing my blog within this framework: *a woman... tentatively exploring the Creator who intelligently and divinely grants her the dignity of free will while laying out a plan for every breath of her life before she was a heartbeat in a living womb.*

> *You see all things; You saw me growing, changing in my mother's womb; Every detail of my life was already written in Your book; You established the length of my life before I ever tasted the sweetness of it.* – Psalm 139:16 VOICE

Writing helps me express grief and establishes fertile spaces for healing. Like a window opened in a musty room, writing for my blog gives my soul access to truth, open and free, like fresh air and sunlight.

...

Reflection:
What activity helps you express yourself?
Where do you find healing?

...

DAY 57

Blog: Blue Sweatshirt Day

I am awake by 6am. My dog, Harley, has let me know he is ready to eat breakfast. The house is cool especially for August. The temperature matches my mood.

I am sad.

I choose the blue sweatshirt from one of many graceful bends in the wrought iron shelf that captures the clothes I will wear again before laundering. This one's hung here awhile, somewhere in the neighborhood of 55 days.

Today is day 57.

I am very sad.

The blue sweatshirt is a well worn men's pull over hoodie, 3X tall, with a splotch of cotton candy pink paint on the left shoulder. When I am honest I know that every day could be a blue sweatshirt day.

The man I loved for 31 years died unexpectedly 57 days ago. I am without my spouse, my friend, my lover... the grumpa to my grandma, the dad to my mom, the husband to my wife, the man to my woman. The person best suited to comfort me in life cannot be here to console me in grief. Every day is a challenge. I find it difficult to breathe.

I remember the day we cleaned out his closet. One of the mourners who came by that weekend commented that a dresser full of clothes remains following the death of her loved one. I snarl and turn away, sensing her condemnation, returning it with my own. Day 2 or day 3 may be too soon, but within my stone-cold heart I hatefully speculate that 3668 days is way too many. Condemnation becomes a tennis match, volleys and drop shots. Only Satan wins.

I pause my writing and laugh aloud now, thinking about the day I added pink paint to the blue sweatshirt. I had volunteered to paint a girl's bedroom in a close friend's home; my husband had been co-volunteered to loft her bed. I had optimistically estimated the painting and drying times, and as we began to loft the bed his shoulder touched a wall. Needless to say the paint was not dry.

It is not the misapplication of cotton candy pink that entices laughter now, it was what happened in the time that followed, a favorite memory of the two of us lying underneath the bed and arguing, fighting about a next step.

I hear another friend come up the steps intent on offering to help. He hears us fighting, senses the tension, and turns to walk back down the stairs without a word. Good man. His arrival and departure invite me back from temporary insanity and I laugh with my husband at the foolishness of this fight.

It was a good day. A very good day.

Blog: Surrender

I run from the sanctuary, exit the building, find myself under a tree. I am undone by the music—a saxophone playing Leonard Cohen's *Hallelujah*, your song, the first one on your playlist, the first song selected as we planned your funeral, the song that drifted through Demmler Park as mourners gathered to celebrate your life.

The invitation to this conference [7] was a gift. This is our second day and it is good to be here.

Leadership Illusions opens with Bill Hybels challenging us to explore our blind spots through introspection, reflection, taking inventory, recreating, re-creating, being with God.

We are invited to reflect on the illusion that growth in leadership capacity and growth in our souls can be achieved simultaneously, that as the leadership curve swoops upward the curve of growth in our souls will keep pace. The truth is that the growth curve of our souls flattens, perhaps turns downward, as in our broken humanity we neglect the spiritual nourishment practices essential to flourishing.

My pen was poised over the designated page in our *Summit Notebook*, my first-born perfectionist ready to meet this challenge. Bill promises beautiful music. A saxophone begins playing… it only takes a few notes for me to recognize the melody… it is your song, the song… *Hallelujah*.

I run from the sanctuary and exit the building. I need to be outside in the open, to feel the sunlight, to see the clouds, to breathe fresh air.

I sit on the bench outside the entrance and give myself over to the messy snotty cries rising up from deep within me, embracing what is illusive and rare for me—a complete surrender to grief.

Time passes. I open my eyes and look up. I see the tree. I lie down on the bench. The shape of the

---

[7] The Global Leadership Summit simulcast, willowcreek.com.

branches above reminds me of the broom tree in Elijah's story.[8]

My tree is mature and young and healthy—flourishing—with rich green leaves and strong limbs. As I kick off my shoes and get more comfortable, I am thankful for the early-morning decision to wear pants instead of a skirt, and find myself embracing the freedom to recline without shocking someone who may walk by—feeling in the moment that even as I dressed this morning God was with me.

Beneath my broom tree I envision my friends continuing on inside the building, the curves on the screen in the sanctuary, my own curves of speed and soul growth. My speed has slowed then flat-lined in the weeks since your death. My soul growth has risen to meet the speed curve then also flat-lined, God weaving the two together for strength and endurance.

In the quiet of surrender I look up and see two large branches that meet, twist—making a knot before separating—one growing toward the sky and the other bowing low to earth. You are the upper branch stretching to understand the universe, eager to learn. I am the lower branch left here on earth, embraced by gravity, caressed by the rain, brushed by the wind, living apart from you.

Abandoning my recent prayers of *please take me too*, I accept God's call back into creation, here on earth for as long as life endures.

---

[8] The biblical story of Elijah is in 1 Kings 16-19, 21-22 and 2 Kings 1-2.

DAY 84

Blog: Finding Rest

An envelope arrived yesterday from the director of the crematory that assisted us in the days following my husband's unexpected death. At first, I did not want to open it, though its thickness indicated it contained material intended to help me, the grieving person. The envelope rests on the kitchen counter for a time, then I retrieve the letter opener—neatness counts—slit open the envelope, remove its contents and read the cover letter. *Dear Renee, During grief, some days are just harder than others. This brochure gives ideas for getting the most from the toughest ones...*

Something in the words acknowledging the toughest days is soothing to my soul. I read every word of the first 8 pages, skip page 9—a list of books—and move onto the brochure. Reading each paragraph, I nod my head in recognition. Yes, me too. Yes. Yes.

The apartment is sometimes empty and unwelcoming. My husband is not here. I am living without sufficient rest. Sleeping during the day is easy enough especially the three days each week I work overnights. Getting into bed alone at a normal time on a normal night triggers weeping. I toss and turn. The sleep that once came so naturally is now illusive. My soul grows weary.

At the same time, I am three journals and three blogs into this journey. Last night I submitted a piece to *Red Tent Living*[9] for possible publication, something I haven't done in months. I am weaving

---

[9] Red Tent Living is an invitation. Amidst all of the impossible, confusing, and shaming ideas of what femininity is in our culture today, we find respite and meaning in gathering together, redtentliving.com.

together thoughts and words in coherent fashion. I am writing and that signals I am on the road to recovering, to finding my new normal. Breakfast with a friend has resumed at Chickadee's; coffee, strategic planning, shared love of God's word with friend-and-pastor has begun again at Caribou.

Today is day 84 and there is renewed hope that someday I will find rest.

[God] heals the brokenhearted and binds up their wounds. – Psalm 147:3

4
Password

Death like an earthquake struck without warning. The sky was sunny this morning, overcast at mid-day, and now in the early evening it is dull gray canvas, ready for the waning sunlight to paint it with color a couple hours from now—sunset 8:36pm.

> **DAY 0**

I sit down at my husband's desk with his cell phone and mine, and prepare to begin making the calls to siblings, though the first call is to a loving and trusted friend, the woman married to our pastor. I hesitate, then leave a voicemail without the euphemisms our society so often wraps around death, choosing instead brief pure words: *Sorry to disturb your vacation ... died this morning, cardiac arrest ... want to celebrate his life sometime Independence Day weekend ... are you available?*

It didn't take long for her to return my call. Overcoming poor cell reception and phones in need of charging, I spoke to her husband too: *yes the holiday weekend works, we could do it sooner ... not necessary, his family will need to travel, long weekend is good.* I hang up and exhale in a loud sigh, wiping away my tears. Now it is time to begin calling his siblings.

My husband and his siblings are tight. When I imagine them as children my mind's eye sees a wall of kids from tallest to smallest, locked arm-in-arm, refusing to let anything break their chain. Gifted, intelligent, logical—the strongest and most focused group of high achievers I've ever encountered—these men and women also love deeply.

I do not want to be the one to break their hearts.

Yet, I will be the one—a requirement of the widow? A way to honor my husband? A gesture of love and respect to his sisters and brothers?

Without taking time to unearth the source of my do-it-yourself insistence, I pick up my husband's cell phone and scroll through his contacts, finding two of the eight siblings. This is unexpected. Now what?

I'm at his desk, so I open his laptop and without hesitating log in with a password he'd shared with me years ago. It works. I do some searching and come up with a couple files that appear to be what I need. I make the first two calls—a brother and a sister. It is awkward at first—as though I needed to prepare a script or checklist or something.

Uncertainty is perched on my shoulder, her beak positioned to peck at me until I submit to her wishes. I feel an overwhelming wave of appreciation for Deb, the sister who called each of her siblings after their mother died this past autumn. She offers to help me. I accept.

You are weak squawks the voice of shame.

. . .

Pause to remember a time when you found yourself floundering in the midst of a task and felt a deep need to be better prepared.

. . .

On some calls I use my husband's cell, hoping that the number will be familiar. On other calls I use my own phone because there is comfort in familiarity, the screen, the locations of the buttons—yet I know that it is highly unlikely my number will be recognized—not because we aren't connected but because my husband was the one who connected us. He made his own calls, sent his own birthday greetings, made the weekend plans for get-togethers with his side of our family.

Chaos is the word that best describes the next two hours. Sometimes my call is answered. Other times it goes to voicemail. The opposite is also true—voicemails left by me prompt callbacks. I do my best to answer and at times I too let a call go to voicemail. In the end I manage to call six of the eight, thankful that Deb, the sister I called first, is making calls too, and saddened that I don't possess the strength to make it through all eight calls. At some point in the night I call my siblings and my parents—exhausted I barely remember making these calls at all.

> My husband was the one who connected us. He made his own calls, sent his own birthday greetings, made the weekend plans for get-togethers with his side of our family.

In the hours, days and weeks that follow, I spend more and more time on my husband's computer—alerting business associates of his death, responding to emails and messages, watching videos with our grandson who wants to be at Grumpa's desk.

> *The LORD is close to the brokenhearted and saves those who are crushed in spirit. – Psalm 34:18*

Gratefulness surrounds me like a soft warm quilt when I realize that our grandson and I were protected and very blessed. Not once did we run into any adult content, images, ads, spam, inappropriate messages, or offensive texts on his computer and cell phone. My husband had been faithful, even in these tempting and private contexts.

I cannot imagine the depth of my despair had it been otherwise. My heart breaks for the men and women whose widowhoods collide with hidden infidelity, adultery and pornography.

. . .

Pause to consider what your loved ones might come across in the wake of your death.
Reflection:
Is now the time for transparency? Is there any behavior that needs to change?

. . .

In a large house some dishes are made of gold or silver, while others are made of wood or clay. Some of these are special, and others are not. [21] That's also how it is with people. The ones who stop doing evil and make themselves pure will become special. Their lives will be holy and pleasing to their Master, and they will be able to do all kinds of good deeds.

[22] Run from temptations that capture young people. Always do the right thing. Be faithful, loving, and easy to get along with. Worship with people whose hearts are pure. – 2 Timothy 2:20-22 CEV

Chapter 5 Widowspeak

5
Laughter

I rise early. Unable to stay in bed any longer, I quietly make coffee. The grandkids are sleeping peacefully; their mom and dad resting. As the coffee brews I find myself pausing to think about the routine of daily life. It doesn't stop for death. It may pause, but it doesn't stop.

DAY 1 I'm scheduled to work a shift Saturday morning, and lead the 9am bible study on Sunday. I pour a mug of fresh coffee and open my online bible to the chapter and verse for Sunday: 1 Peter 3. Reading the first few words I can hear my husband's laughter. He is laughing with two friends from church, guys a bit older than him who died this past year. It feels as though they are looking over my shoulder and enjoying this way too much:

> *Wives, in the same way submit yourselves to your own husbands so that, if any of them do not believe the word, they may be won over without words by the behavior of their wives, [2] when they see the purity and reverence of your lives. [3] Your beauty should not come from outward adornment, such as elaborate hairstyles and the wearing of gold jewelry or fine clothes. [4] Rather, it should be that of your inner self, the unfading beauty of a gentle and quiet spirit, which is of great worth in God's sight. [5] For this is the way the holy women of the past who put*

their hope in God used to adorn themselves. They submitted themselves to their own husbands, [6] like Sarah, who obeyed Abraham and called him her lord. You are her daughters if you do what is right and do not give way to fear. – 1 Peter 3:1-6

As a woman and a wife, I was not all that good at submission. It took me a long, long time. I laugh along with my husband and our friends—a shared laughter of recognition and appreciation. And, the laughter lifts my heavy heart.

. . .

Reflection:
Husbands, what does a wife's submission look like for you? How does it feel?
Wives, what prompts us to withhold our trust? How does it feel to submit?

. . .

DAY 0

I laughed yesterday too, the day he died. As inappropriate as it may seem, there is a moment after the Q&A and my desperate prayer for a miracle, a point where conversation returns to an uncharted normal. We are waiting for the coroner when someone asks about my husband's health.

I reply: *Just a few days ago he built the fire-escape platform on the second story of this duplex. He was up and down the ladder like a squirrel. He had just seen his cardiologist, and except for being told to lose the 15 pounds he'd gained, everything was good to go.*

Someone in the room quips: *I'd ask for a refund.*

I laugh aloud, responding: *The bill hasn't even arrived yet.* And for me there is comfort in the normalcy of laughter.

In *Processing Through Grief* Stephanie Jose writes: *It might be easier to be around a grieving person who holds back their emotions, but there is very little benefit to this emotional self-control except making everyone around you more comfortable. Your job while grieving is not to be thinking about how to make everyone else more comfortable ...* [10]

> Your job while grieving is not to be thinking about how to make everyone else more comfortable.

...

Pause to remember a time when you experienced difficulty caring for yourself.
Reflection:
How did you overcome?

...

They devoted themselves to the apostles' teaching and to fellowship, to the breaking of bread and to prayer. [43] Everyone was filled with awe at the many wonders and signs performed by the apostles. [44] All the believers were together and had everything in common. [45] They sold property and possessions to give to anyone who had need. [46] Every day they continued to meet together in the temple courts. They broke bread in their homes and ate together with glad and sincere hearts, [47] praising God and enjoying the favor of all the people. And the Lord added to their number daily those who were being saved. – Acts 2:42-47

---

[10] *Processing Through Grief: Guided Exercises to Understand Your Emotions and Recover From Loss* by Stephanie Jose, LMHC, LCAT. Foreword by Cécile Rêve, LMHC.

Chapter 6 Widowspeak

6

Obituary

Rewind 2007: I had been without a church for ten years when two coworkers invited me to theirs and one Sunday I walked into the community that is Fellowship. For weeks each Sunday morning I cried tears of deep acceptance, experiencing a sense of coming home, an inexpressible joy.

Once the tears stopped, I skipped *The 7 Habits* and began with a borrowed copy of *The 8th*.[11] At the suggestion of our pastor all around me friends were writing their eulogies, and I was weirdly stuck thinking about my obituary. Dates, names, spouse, children, siblings, in-laws, parents, workplace, hobbies. Obituary is math, in print, black and white. One photograph.

Eulogy is so much more. Eulogy is what we hope for, the desires held within our human hearts.[12]

For decades I'd worked in the printing industry, quick turn-around shops catering to businesses, where the focus was on quality, profit, meeting deadlines, keeping promises. Funeral directors were professional and courteous customers. Accuracy and timeliness emerged as critical. Grieving people hold little capacity for errors and there is no margin for missed deadlines.

Real Time Day 1: Overnight I appropriated most of the dates and names from his mother's obituary, and had already included

---

[11] *The 7 Habits of Highly Effective People: Powerful Lessons in Personal Change* and *The 8th Habit: From Effectiveness to Greatness,* Stephen R. Covey, author.
[12] *My Eulogy* published in my blog in March 2012, is included in *Resources*.

them in a Microsoft *Word* document by the time I arrive at the cremation society on Friday at 10:35am.

DAY 1

I am late. I had not called. Everyone else is already here—our daughter, our son and our daughter-in-law. The man who had given me his business card in the quiet of the back yard greets us, then seats us in a conference room. Coffee and water are offered, perhaps soda. We sit down and begin the unfamiliar process. Practical things, the cost of cremation, burial, urn, casket, death notice, obituary ... the lists complete and quite extensive are laid out calmly, simply, slowly.

The dates and names I had pulled together needed one more thing, the essential paragraph that brings the person to life. Confident we could do this and trusting that my heart would know the right words when I heard them, I began with an example: *He enjoyed beating his wife [pause] at Scrabble.*[13]

We laughed. He did enjoy beating me at Scrabble. Though it is in poor taste to pause and imply violence, this one sentence and the laughter that follows disperses the tension. Each person contributes something honoring, humorous, life affirming, and we add this paragraph to the dates and names already gathered:

[He] enjoyed beating his wife at Scrabble and riding his bicycle up the hills even after he quit riding on RAGBRAI. As a young father he was savvy in science and won his daughter's respect by recalling the speed of light faster than her middle school science teacher. He taught his son by example how to be a good man and a good father. Babies and toddlers were inexplicably drawn to him; dandelions feared him.

If you knew him in daily life you'd probably witnessed the babies and toddlers in action. In places like grocery stores, shopping malls and company picnics, young kids would literally

---

[13] Scrabble® is a game my paternal grandmother played with me and my cousins, one I played often with my husband, and a joy I hope to one day share with our grandchildren.

walk away from their parents or caregivers, come up to my husband and touch him on the leg or take his hand. He loved kids and kids knew it. Babies would fall asleep in his arms, listening to his heartbeat and the sound of his breathing, snuggling into his calm strength.

...

Think about your own obituary and eulogy.
Reflection:
What are the things likely to be included?
What are the strengths you want to be remembered for?
What will be your legacy?

...

The dandelion comment is purely humorous and decidedly historic. In 1995 we moved for his career and happened to buy a house next to an organic gardener. She urged us not to use a lawn service and instead to pull the dandelions. What at first seemed like an odd request eventually became part of our tradition. The dad-powered four-foot-long dandelion fork actually worked, and once grandchildren arrived on the scene we experienced a renewed appreciation for this earth-friendly alternative to chemically treating for a weed-free lawn. No dandelions—ever. Did dandelions fear him? It doesn't matter. The point is to remember and celebrate. People who'd spent any amount of time at our house likely knew this about him, his passion for a dandelion-free lawn. These three words—dandelions feared him—held joy!

The obituary reflects the life my husband lived. We move on. There are decisions to make, other tasks to accomplish. Urns are displayed in another room. A casket isn't necessary. We look and talk and decide. Because he and I had set aside time and shared our wishes, this section of the unfamiliar post-death journey is surprisingly straightforward.

As our time at the cremation society comes to a close, our funeral director gently lets us know that my husband's body is available for viewing if anyone needs or wants to see him, including the grandchildren, if that would be helpful. There is some hesitation; silence, then a *yes but not alone*, from our daughter-in-law; another *yes* from our daughter agreeing to join her; an additional moment or two of silence, then a *yes* from our son. I choose to remain in the conference room.

For our children the private viewing of an un-retouched body is a beautiful way to begin saying good-bye to the man who'd loved being Dad.

. . .

Reflection:
Do you like dark or milk chocolate? Coffee or tea?
What is your favorite flower, herb or seed?
Your favorite color? Season? Sport?
How do you spend your time? Your money?
What are your passions? Who do you love?
What does your end of life celebration look like?
What do you want included?
How do you want to be remembered?

. . .

"Therefore I tell you, do not worry about your life, what you will eat or drink; or about your body, what you will wear. Is not life more than food, and the body more than clothes? ^{26} Look at the birds of the air; they do not sow or reap or store away in barns, and yet your heavenly Father feeds them. Are you not much more valuable than they? ^{27} Can any one of you by worrying add a single hour to your life?"

^{28} "And why do you worry about clothes? See how the flowers of the field grow. They do not labor or spin. ^{29} Yet I tell you that not even Solomon in all his splendor was dressed like one of these. ^{30} If that is how God clothes the grass of the field, which is here today and tomorrow is thrown into the fire, will he not much more clothe you—you of little faith? ^{31} So do not worry, saying, 'What shall we eat?' or 'What shall we drink?' or 'What shall we wear?' ^{32} For the pagans run after all these things, and your heavenly Father knows that you need them. ^{33} But seek first his kingdom and his righteousness, and all these things will be given to you as well. ^{34} Therefore do not worry about tomorrow, for tomorrow will worry about itself. Each day has enough trouble of its own." – Matthew 6:25-34

7
Unbalanced

My husband and I were at the tail end of the 9.3 million Americans losing homes in the Great Recession.

The market for my husband's business services—developing and overseeing the construction of office buildings, water park hotels and shopping centers—has dried up. He takes a job in a local sand mine, walking several miles a day to collect and test quality samples. On the day the county sheriff holds the foreclosure auction of our home, the employees at the sand mine are given notice. There is no more work. Our household income plummets from struggling middle class to economically impoverished where we remain for seven months.

Early in the foreclosure process I receive a gift from our pastor and friend, a coping tool, H.A.L.T. Am I Hungry, Angry, Lonely, or Tired?

If so, in those moments when I feel like lashing out, do I desire instead to halt, to choose not to speak? This is wisdom, good advice, a sturdy four-pronged approach. Step back and assess before responding. Practice self-control.

If H.A.L.T. is a four-legged stool in times of economic stress, in the days and weeks following my husband's death my slightly wobbly stool is now wretchedly unstable. It is missing a leg. I am desperately lonely, unprepared for the little everyday things that can unlock heartache. Each unanticipated blow triggers a freefall, the sensation of tipping, falling and tumbling emotionally to the floor, grief stricken and unable to cope.

The first freefall is triggered by a voicemail on my husband's phone, a message left by the city billing office asking for health insurance information for the 9-1-1 response. A routine inquiry—except that he had DIED. I am unprepared, shocked and isolated by this blunt reminder, irritated that his death has not been noted in this context. The feeling of being all alone in the world comes crashing in as though someone unseen had jumped out at me then doused me with a bucket of ice cold water. I sit shivering, my husband's cell phone in my hand.

Hungry? Yes and no. Despite the bags of cheese puffs and packages of brand name chocolate sandwich cookies dropped off by friends and family, I am not eating much at all, not even my favorite junk foods. People bring crock pots of things more substantial, but these cook then cool then pile up in the refrigerator. A friend I trust with my helplessness comes over after worship one Sunday to deal with the leftover food. I stop at a grocery store and purchase 16, perhaps 20, storage containers. The amount of food is that overwhelming. Or, more accurately, it is that overwhelming to me. It takes my friend about 30 minutes to clean up. She uses just a few of the many too many containers I'd purchased. What seemed insurmountable is in reality three food-filled crock pots. *This is not who I am* cries the silent broken me from somewhere deep inside. The possibility that I am losing my grip on sanity becomes a constant companion, an unsettling and unwelcome sensation.

> The possibility that I am losing my grip on sanity becomes a constant companion, an unsettling and unwelcome sensation.

Angry? No and yes. I didn't experience anger at God, or anger at the man who'd been my husband. My anger, when it surfaces, is at the people who claim to love me then hurt me most deeply.

Despite 28 hours of open visitation in our back yard—a few hours each afternoon for six days—some people seem to feel they are entitled to more.

DAY 8

Choosing to come uninvited and without waiting for me to return their phone call, a man and a woman show up at the apartment. It is a cool and sunny spring morning with just a hint of summer. I've gone to the bank and plan to do a couple other errands if I feel up to it. While I am out I receive a call from the cremation society. My husband's cremains are ready. Did I want to pick them up? Yes, I decide. Now is as good a time as any.

At some point along the way, I receive a text alerting me that people are at the apartment. I avoid going home. I avoid going home until I can't stand to avoid it any longer. When I turn onto our street, I see that there is not room for my car in our driveway. I parallel park down the street a block. All I want to do is lie down on a bed and weep. This task—picking up my husband's ashes—has crushed me.

Too weak to make small talk or even come face-to-face with the uninvited guests, I leave my husband's ashes in the back seat of the car and walk down our street and up the driveway. Uncertain exactly what to do—yet certain I do not want to go into the apartment—I pull a lawn chair to the shadiest corner of the back yard, the corner where lush grass meets nine acres of woods. I sit down to weep.

Our grandson is the first to come to me. He asks why I am sad. He responds in a way that only a three-year-old can, with purity of heart and the compassion of a tiny hand reaching out to comfort me. No hesitation. No shame. Grumpa had been his Bestie too.

Lonely? Yes, yes, yes. The depth and breadth of the hole created in my life when my husband died is indescribable. I find myself without my spouse, my friend, my lover, the grumpa to my grandma, the dad to my mom, the husband to my wife, the man to my woman. The apartment is too quiet, the nights too long, the days filled with an unfamiliar cadence. Simple things, like washing the sheets, remain undone. In my ordinary life bedding is washed weekly. In this new reality I go 55 days before finding the strength to accomplish the task. Lonely is the missing leg on my stool. I am lonely all the time.

Tired? Yes and no and yes. When life slows down in a way that sheets remain unwashed, there is ample time to sleep. The guestroom, where I'd slept—or not slept—since the day he died, even has daylight curtains. Day or night, light isn't an issue. Neither is noise. The upstairs apartment in this old house duplex is vacant. Our daughter and I had begun to paint and she is installing new flooring, so for now I am the only tenant in the whole place.

When this misadventure began I was at a new job, scheduled for early morning training shifts, 22 hours a week, manageable. In the time between my husband's death and the celebration of his life, training ends and work becomes unmanageable—40 hours a week, third shift. I work two nights, then miss three. Sleep that once came naturally is now illusive. Even when I am not working, getting into bed alone at a normal time on a normal night triggers weeping. I toss and turn, restless long into the night.

Sleeplessness eventually becomes insomnia peaking 99 days after I become a widow. I am easily frustrated and verbally abusive. Our daughter takes my dog, Harley, overnight. I know in my heart it is possible I might hurt him. I miss another shift at work. The team leaders and others are phenomenally supportive, respecting my need for privacy, encouraging me to rest when I call in.

While I want to avoid thinking about the uninvited guests who occupied my living room the morning I picked up my husband's ashes, it is sweet to remember that just a few hours later a beautiful bouquet of fresh fragrant flowers arrived—a gift from my employer with a card signed by the team leaders. Perfect timing.

...

*Pause to remember a time when difficulty and
blessing simultaneously impacted you.*

...

DAY 19

On a Tuesday morning, 19 days after my husband's death, I am meeting with our friend and pastor, the man who just a few short months ago gave me H.A.L.T. He is back from sabbatical and his family vacation. He buys me breakfast. It is time to prepare for the celebration of my husband's life. We go over details: song, song, song, song … widow arrives, song, welcome, reading *Ps 5:1-7*, reading *Ps 90:1-6, 13-17*; eulogy 1 and eulogy 2, song, reading *John 11:17-44*, pastoral reflection, invite thoughts from guests, invite to lunch, closing song, then song, song, song… a mid-summer Saturday at a neighborhood park just a few blocks from the apartment, 2pm, rain or shine. There is only one question I cannot fully answer: why I left out *John 11:1-16*.

> *A man named Lazarus was sick. He lived in Bethany with his sisters, Mary and Martha. ² This is the Mary who later poured the expensive perfume on the Lord's feet and wiped them with her hair. Her brother, Lazarus, was sick. ³ So the two sisters sent a message to Jesus telling him, "Lord, your dear friend is very sick."*
>
> *⁴ But when Jesus heard about it he said, "Lazarus's sickness will not end in death. No, it happened for the glory of God so that the Son of God will receive glory from this." ⁵ So although Jesus loved Martha, Mary, and Lazarus, ⁶ he stayed where he was for the next two days. ⁷ Finally, he said to his disciples, "Let's go back to Judea."*

> *⁸ But his disciples objected. "Rabbi," they said, "only a few days ago the people in Judea were trying to stone you. Are you going there again?"*
> *⁹ Jesus replied, "There are twelve hours of daylight every day. During the day people can walk safely. They can see because they have the light of this world. ¹⁰ But at night there is danger of stumbling because they have no light." ¹¹ Then he said, "Our friend Lazarus has fallen asleep, but now I will go and wake him up."*
> *¹² The disciples said, "Lord, if he is sleeping, he will soon get better!" ¹³ They thought Jesus meant Lazarus was simply sleeping, but Jesus meant Lazarus had died.*
> *¹⁴ So he told them plainly, "Lazarus is dead. ¹⁵ And for your sakes, I'm glad I wasn't there, for now you will really believe. Come, let's go see him."*
> *¹⁶ Thomas, nicknamed the Twin, said to his fellow disciples, "Let's go, too—and die with Jesus."*
> – John 11:1-16 NLT

Death as an opportunity to believe? The journey as chance to die with Jesus? A promise that Lazarus' sickness will not end in death? I am comforted that Jesus' disciples didn't always fully believe. I am inspired that Thomas, the man we often dismiss as *doubting Thomas*, is brave.

I am delighted that Mary's gift of perfuming Jesus' feet will be revealed as flawless.

> *"Leave her alone," Jesus replied. "It was intended that she should save this perfume for the day of my burial. ⁸You will always have the poor among you, but you will not always have me."* – John 12:7-8

8

Day 23

The man whose life we are celebrating is a man I met in a bar after midnight. We met in a bar after midnight just a few short weeks after my husband of nearly four years left me for the sixteen-year-old who would become his second wife. I was an ancient 23 years old. The 1980s world around me pounded a steady drumbeat: *this will not end well.*

I was surrounded—a society of selfishness and greed, the pessimistic authors of articles on relationships, the twisted statistic that 50% of marriages end in divorce, and the people who'd known me for years fully believing and saying aloud: *this relationship will not last, this is foolishness, he can't be trusted.*

Decades later I am in a neighborhood park, seated in the front row—me, the widow—surrounded by family and friends, all the people dearest to me, except one—the man we are celebrating, the man God designed for me. My brother-in-law, the man married to my sister, steps out in front of the crowd gathered here. He and my husband married into the family, became husbands and uncles, for better or worse—companions and conspirators attempting to avoid the ongoing drama of three adult female siblings and our offspring, five girls and three boys. Hunting and fishing are my brother-in-law's passions. George takes the microphone. He speaks of my husband and our son, the adventures and misadventures, tells stories of hunting and fishing. There is laughter. He speaks of the years his youngest daughters spent time at our house after school, my husband supervising from his home office, the freezer and cupboard filled with the girls' favorite foods because my husband did our grocery shopping and cared deeply enough to remember. He speaks of my husband and my daughter, the relationship, a father's love.

And my mind drifts. I remember my husband and my brother-in-law—two men so different and so alike—disassembling a chain-link dog kennel, loading it in a pickup truck and transporting it to the local high school for the set of *West Side Story*.

. . .

Reflection:
When the time comes, who do you see holding the
microphone or stepping up to the
lectern to give your eulogy?

. . .

A few minutes later, my husband's sister is the one standing on the grass facing me and other mourners. Janet is holding the microphone, giving an impromptu eulogy in lieu of the one prepared by another sibling—a brother delayed by heavy traffic. Another sister joins her. Deb and Janet tell stories of childhood, reveal the charm of their brother, his kindness and love, childhood joys and struggles.

Janet—the sister whose family he stayed with when he first arrived in Dallas, TX—talks about the summer he and I met. I encourage her to reveal the details, the bar… after midnight… to tell the story with transparency, without shame. The cloud of witnesses, our fellow mourners, includes a strong showing of people from Fellowship church. There will be no condemnation. The story is known. My husband stood in front of them one Christmas Eve, not all that long ago, as we explored the birth of Jesus from Joseph's perspective. My husband told our church as he looked at me: *I loved her first*.

Later, in the warmth of a fading summer day so filled with sadness, Janet and I stand outside the apartment door in a back yard filled with family and friends. She shares with me the words my heart needs to hear: *Ben called us that summer, saying he'd met a great girl, then shared with us another joy—the kids.*

Yes, I knew. And, yes, I needed to know again. My wounded heart had never quite relaxed into trusting that I was worthy of his love.[14]

July 2nd—the day we celebrate his life—is Day 23 in this journey of death.

. . .

Reflection:
Where do you find your heart not trusting?
Where do you feel unworthy of love?

. . .

For we do not have a high priest who is unable to sympathize with our weaknesses, but one who in every respect has been tempted as we are, yet without sin. [16] *Let us then with confidence draw near to the throne of grace, that we may receive mercy and find grace to help in time of need.*
— Hebrews 4:15-16 ESV

---

[14] In the teachings of Dan B. Allender, PhD, my heart discovered great healing. Dan Allender and Tremper Longman's GOD LOVES SEX is especially delightful and the only book I ever purchased that my husband voluntarily picked up from the dining room table then finished reading before I did!

9
Lists

I feel powerless. The uninvited guests who had waited in the apartment on the day I picked up my husband's ashes betray me, betray my husband—one chooses not to attend the funeral, the other speaks of my husband's death as a suicide to someone who chooses to tell someone, who chooses to tell ... until someone told me in the midst of the celebration of his life.

Three weeks later, there is a nagging, frustrated, internal scream *Hear My No!*—followed by the wish to savagely terminate communication with everyone, even the most thoughtful mourners. I want to silence the authors who wrote all those books and blogs recommending recurrent and continued contact. I simply want to be left alone, unencumbered, submerged in my pain.

> I simply want to be left alone, unencumbered, submerged in my pain.

DAY 44 At this point I am nearing the end of my first 96-page journal. In addition to what I am reading from the bible, I am journaling through *Processing Through Grief* by Stephanie Jose.[15] On this particular day I am reflecting on the biblical story in which Judas is critical of Mary using her perfume on Jesus' feet.

---

[15] *Processing Through Grief*, Ibid.

Six days before the Passover, Jesus came to Bethany, where Lazarus lived, whom Jesus had raised from the dead. ² Here a dinner was given in Jesus' honor. Martha served, while Lazarus was among those reclining at the table with him. ³ Then Mary took about a pint of pure nard, an expensive perfume; she poured it on Jesus' feet and wiped his feet with her hair. And the house was filled with the fragrance of the perfume.

⁴ But one of his disciples, Judas Iscariot, who was later to betray him, objected, ⁵ "Why wasn't this perfume sold and the money given to the poor? It was worth a year's wages."

⁶ He did not say this because he cared about the poor but because he was a thief; as keeper of the money bag, he used to help himself to what was put into it.

⁷ "Leave her alone," Jesus replied. "It was intended that she should save this perfume for the day of my burial. ⁸You will always have the poor among you, but you will not always have me."

– John 12:1-8

My journal reads: *I feel as though the following people are critical of me, eight names... or need something from me, six names ... or can't be trusted, eight names.*

Then, something good emerges. I write*: safe people? three names... then two more, then more names. Look at that list, 23 safe people! Wow! I am so blessed!*

Welcome to my rollercoaster.

DAY 46

A couple days after putting down on paper the lists of names, my scratchy handwriting[16] reveals my toxic mood—*explosive emotional outburst—pain, hate, blame, resentment, rage, jealousy, confusion, fear, impatient, tense, agitated, frustrated, overwhelmed, reactive, powerless.*

Four words stand out:
- ✓ *pain*
- ✓ *resentment*
- ✓ *confusion*
- ✓ *overwhelmed.*

I write: *I am angry that he died too soon. I am angry that his life was diminished by others' greed. I am angry that I feel vulnerable and alone.*

On the next page I continue: *I am angry that so much of my time between his death and the celebration of his life was spent being a grief counselor for others. I am angry that those who claimed to love me most put me at the periphery of their pain rather than at the center of their love.*

Ugly, dark, hateful words. Even as I write, I do not want to share the truth, how bitter I am in my widowhood. *Shhh don't tell* taunts me; the familiar voice of shame.

---

[16] My journals contain several styles of cursive handwriting reflecting the scattered state of my mind and heart.

Prayer

Dearest Jesus,

You wept at the death of Lazarus and taught that all who mourn shall be comforted. Grant me the comfort of your presence in my loss. Send your Holy Spirit to direct me lest I make hasty or foolish decisions. Send your Holy Spirit to give me courage lest through fear I recoil from living. Send your Holy Spirit to bring me your peace lest bitterness, false guilt, or regret take root in my heart. The Lord has given. The Lord has taken away. Blessed be the name of the Lord. Amen.[17]

A List of Words

In my journeys through *Wounded Heart*[18] and my on-going travels within *The Elijah Project*[19] I discovered that words to express ourselves are vital to the healing process. Whether you are a writer or not, words will help you and those you love name what you are experiencing. The words listed here are loosely gathered around the concepts of fear, anger, anxiousness, sadness, ambivalence and joy.

· · ·

Choose 3 to 5 words to describe what you are experiencing.
Explore the nuances of your words.
Reflection:
What feels familiar? What is unexpected?
What is God revealing? What is God redeeming?

· · ·

---

[17] Adapted from *Prayer in Time of Bereavement,* catholic.org.
[18] *Wounded Heart: Hope for Adult Victims of Childhood Sexual Abuse* by Dan B. Allender, PhD. Foreword by Larry Crabb, PhD.
[19] *The Elijah Project* series by Andrea M. Polnaszek, LCSW.

FEAR
Abandoned
Aghast
Alarmed
Apologetic
Apprehensive
Bound
Careful
Cautious
Closed
Clueless
Cutoff
Defined
Deserted
Desperate
Disconnected
Dismayed
Disoriented
Dread
Edgy
Exposed
Fearful
Frantic
Frightened
Haunted
Horrified
Indefensible
Inferior
Insane
Insanity
Insecure
Intimidated

Insufficient
Isolated
Masked
Mortified
Nervous
Panicked
Perplexed
Petrified
Polite
Powerless
Puzzled
Ruffled
Scared
Self-conscious
Separated
Shunned
Stunned
Surprised
Surrounded
Tense
Terrified
Uninformed
Withdrawn

ANGER
Aggressive
Agitated
Angry
Annoyed
Betrayed
Bitter
Bristling
Chagrined

Challenged
Critical
Criticized
Defiled
Degraded
Demanding
Embittered
Enraged
Explosive
Fed up
Frustrated
Fuming
Furious
Harsh
Hatred
Hell bent
Impatient
Incensed
Inconsiderate
Indignant
Infuriated
Irate
Irked
Irritated
Jealous
Oppressed
Outraged
Perturbed
Rage
Rejected
Restricted
Rigid

Sharp
Shocked
Steamed
Strained
Ticked off
Trivialized
Unkind
Unreasonable
Violated

ANXIOUSNESS

Ashamed
Awkward
Baffled
Belittled
Burned
Chaotic
Clumsy
Confused
Detached
Dirty
Disgusted
Displeased
Dissatisfied
Dumb
Dumbfounded
Embarrassed
Fidgety
Flustered
Foolish
Guilty
Humiliated
Ignored

Illegitimate
Imperfect
Ineffective
Inhibited
Insignificant
Jumbled
Pathetic
Repulsed
Shamed
Traumatized
Weak
Worthless

SADNESS

Abbreviated
Absent
Abnormal
Adrift
Alone
Amputated
Bewildered
Broken
Crazy
Crushed
Dazed
Deep
Defeated
Dejected
Depressed
Desolate
Despairing
Devastated
Disappointed

Disengaged
Disheartened
Disrupted
Distracted
Distressed
Down
Downhearted
Drowning
Empty
Excluded
Exhausted
Extinguished
Forgotten
Fluid
Forsaken
Fragile
Fragmented
Gloomy
Glum
Grieved
Helpless
Hopeless
Hungering
Impaired
Incomplete
Irrelevant
Less than
Lonely
Lonesome
Lost
Lousy
Low

Meek	Uneasy	Uncertain
Melancholy	Unfit	Unsure
Mournful	Unfocused	Unresolved
Muddled	Unhappy	Vacillating
Neglected	Unhinged	Warring
Numb	Unimportant	Wavering
Out of place	Unlovable	Wondering
Outcast	Unqualified	**JOY**
Overlooked	Unsettled	Able
Overwhelmed	Unwanted	Accepted
Pained	Unwelcome	Adequate
Messy	Valueless	Adventurous
Practical	Vulnerable	Affirmed
Pragmatic	Weary	Anchored
Punished	Worn out	Appreciative
Reclusive	Wretched	At ease
Regretful	**AMBIVALENCE**	Available
Remorseful	Clashing	Bold
Remote	Complicated	Brave
Removed	Contradictory	Buoyed
Retreating	Debatable	Calm
Shaken	Doubtful	Capable
Sick	Equivocal	Casual
Small	Extraneous	Changed
Somber	Fickle	Changing
Sorry	Fluctuating	Cheerful
Submerged	Hesitant	Cherished
Torn	Inconclusive	Clever
Unable	Irresolute	Comfortable
Unarmed	Mixed	Comforted
Unavailable	Opposed	Compassionate
Uncomfortable	Silent	Competent

Connected	Healing	Proud
Considerate	Heard	Purposed
Contented	Honest	Qualified
Courageous	Humorous	Quiet
Cradled	Important	Reasonable
Creative	Informed	Receptive
Curious	Inspired	Refreshed
Delighted	Joyful	Relaxed
Determined	Kind	Relevant
Discerning	Learning	Rhythmic
Ecstatic	Legitimate	Robust
Elated	Lifted	Sane
Embraced	Listening	Satisfied
Encouraged	Love	Secure
Energetic	Loveable	Seen
Engaged	Loved	Settled
Equipped	Lulled	Skillful
Exhilarated	Mellow	Spirited
Expectant	Mighty	Stable
Familiar	Moored	Still
Fearless	Natural	Strong
Fit	Nesting	Supported
Flourishing	Nice	Sure
Focused	Nostalgic	Thankful
Free	Nurtured	Thrilled
Generous	Open	Trusting
Gentle	Optimistic	Truthful
Giddy	Overjoyed	Wanted
Grateful	Passionate	Warm
Grounded	Peaceful	Welcome
Happy	Powerful	Whole
Healed	Precious	Wise

10

Sex

Shhh don't tell hisses loudest here, in this chapter titled *Sex*. There are those who will read this and not want me to talk about the intimacy between a wife and her husband, between me and my husband.

Is it because we met in a bar after midnight? Is it because our first day together began in the awkwardness of the morning after? Is it because the man I miss the most is the man who was my lover?

Even as our aging bodies began to betray us the intimacy of being man and woman—husband and wife—remained. I am a morning person; he a night owl. We made it work. I liked to take an afternoon nap, so he took time away from his work to spend the occasional afternoon in bed with me. He kissed me goodnight even when he had to wake me because I'd gone to bed too early.

The deepest sorrow is that I miss his touch, his embrace, being quiet together, the comfort, the pillow talk. I miss the shape of his hands, his laughter, his intelligence, his presence.

In the days following his death a piece I'd written yet never published surfaced—*Blue Flannel LAX*. I read it and wept, put it aside, rediscovered it, read it and wept, put it aside again.

I was so broken. He loved me anyway.

Blue Flannel LAX [20]

I don't recognize him when I get off the plane at LAX. He is there in the crowd, the mob of people waiting at the gate for the passengers arriving from a snowy MSP to the sunshine of LAX. Wow. He's much better looking than I remember. So tall!

He's wearing a blue and black flannel shirt, a heavy cotton-wool blend, one of the shirts I snuggled into when we were together back in Wisconsin, an oversized men's shirt, making me feel delicate, small, cared for, safe.

The past eight months have been such a long year. I am exhausted, torn between job and daycare, meeting strangers in bars and loving this man—a man 2,000 miles away.

My $6.50 an hour good job isn't cutting it. My estranged husband has a new family, his girlfriend and her son. She's quite lovely, all of sixteen, from his hometown.

I am exhausted. I struggle to make the rent. On the weekends when the kids are with my soon-to-be-ex and I am alone, I spend way too much money on booze.

My ex-husband and I called it quits a week or two before our June wedding anniversary. We would have been married four years. Our children, a boy and a girl, are six months and twenty-one months old—two babies in diapers. Childcare is expensive. Rent. Food. Bills. Stress. Demands. It all piles up. Not much time to nurture each other, care for each

---

[20] Written in 2008 *Blue Flannel LAX* reveals my struggle, the chaos of divorce, economic poverty, single motherhood, promiscuity, public shame and private fear—the broken person I was when God brought Ben to me.

other, love each other. We both work. We can't pay our bills.

We sit at the kitchen table and hammer out the details, an agreement of how this will work. There is no money for attorneys. We write down a shared custody agreement, split our stuff. He takes the kids and goes to stay with his parents. I close down the apartment, let the pregnant young woman who cares for our children know we will no longer need her. She was so very good with the children. She cared for all of us.

I am angry. He is angry. A few days before he leaves, we are fighting, clawing at each others' hearts and heads with sharp words. I am out of control. He holds me against the refrigerator with his left arm, pulls back his right hand, forming a fist, ready to punch me. I take a breath and find that I am deadly calm in the moment. *You are only going to hit me once,* I hiss, my eyes fixed coldly on his.

He lets me go. Defeated. Exhausted. Would I have done this divorce thing differently if he had hit me? Would I have made the mistake of letting him take my children to his parents' home on the flimsy kitchen-table agreement we put together for ending our marriage?

His parents, his family, hire an attorney—not just any attorney, the best divorce attorney available. I hire an attorney too, one I thought I could afford. As Julia Roberts' character will say in *Pretty Woman* to the Rodeo Drive sales associates who'd refused to help her: *Big mistake. Huge.*[21]

---

[21] *Pretty Woman* (1990) starring Richard Geer and Julia Roberts.

I move into the two bedroom trailer of a friend. She too is in the midst of divorce, wanting to make a home for her children. In letting me move in, she forfeits her dream: a bedroom for her three boys.

I am a terrible roommate. Selfish. Careless. We drink a little at Wagner's—a local bar. We own the shot glasses that declare it.

There are men, lots of men. It is the 1980s. Pre-AIDS. Promiscuity reigns. Wagner's has three bars. On the weekends the bar on the lower level has live country music. Upstairs, the band plays rock-n-roll. Years later when someone uses the word *slut*, I will ask aloud: *How many? Could you put a number on that?*

My number is 23. I take pleasure in making a person like this uncomfortable, watching them squirm in the realization that he—or she—just called me a slut. At some point toward the end of my 23 conquests, trophies, shames, men—I am in the country bar, pissed as hell at men and life and God.

. . .

Pause to remember a time when
you were angry with God.
Reflection:
What did it take for you to let go?
What did it take for you to heal?

. . .

I am waiting for the married bartender who is— in my experience—willing. I am not interested in the game. If I was looking for someone new tonight I'd be upstairs listening to rock-n-roll. I really don't care much for country music. Hatred oozes from my pores, the word *bitch* is like a neon sign flashing on my forehead.

A messily-divorcing-twenty-something-brunette sits in a too-familiar local bar, her children visiting the soon-to-be-ex and his girlfriend this July 4th weekend. She simply wants to be left alone.

A tall man walks over, asks in a Texas accent, "Y'all mind if I sit here?"

Her reply is caustically dismissive: "You can sit anywhere you want."

She returns to her drink, is surprised—shocked actually—when he sits down. The scene is dark, lacking the sparkling hope of magic storybook endings.

. . .

Reflection:
What is the beauty of believing in storybook endings?
What is the danger?

. . .

I go with him—this Texan—to his apartment. In the morning I am fairly certain he does not remember my name. He is smooth to the point of arrogant—handing me a Rolodex® card as he asks for my phone number.

He actually calls and I am surprised—shocked actually—again. We see a play, go to a baseball game, eat meals together, enjoy sex. His nickname is Ben. He grew up in Iowa, picked up the accent working in Dallas, TX.

By fall the woman who shares her trailer with me is not happy. That makes two of us. We are both hurting so much. Life is breaking us. We cannot heal fast enough to stop the bleeding in our souls.

    I move out, take an apartment in an old school building, something I think I can afford … a place I cannot afford. When her new place falls away, she moves in with me, into the bedroom intended for my kids.

. . .

Reflection:
Describe a time that for you resonates
with the idea that life is breaking us, that we are
bleeding in our souls.

. . .

    Later that autumn, living in the apartment I can't afford, I swallow my pride and ask Ben for help. My daughter's birthday is coming up. I can't pay my electric bill. He gives me money to pay the utilities, shows up with toys for my daughter, toys for my son, a lamp for their nursery, bags of stuff.

    Ben is with us at Christmas. We take a photo— he and I with the kids, my daughter hugging an irresistible Dalmatian. In a few days my son will be one year old. And, Ben will be transferred to Los Angeles.

    He will send flowers for my January birthday. The card will read: *Life's a beach without you.*

    We agree that it is foolish to expect commitment when we are living so far apart, when our relationship is so new, when my divorce is still in the works. He's scheduled to return in April or May. It is possible that he will not return, that the California office will offer him a permanent position.

We agree to see other people. We agree to stay in touch.

I go back into the bars. My friend—the roommate from the two bedroom trailer—is by my side. One night she turns and says to me: *He's not here.*

Who's not here? I ask.

Ben. The man you're looking for. Ben's not here.

She is right. The man I am looking for is not in the bars. He is standing in the crowd at the gate as I get off the plane at LAX.

We spend the weekend together. He puts me back on the plane and I return to my life in the cold Wisconsin winter.

My apartment is too expensive. My estranged husband and his attorney are dragging their feet. I can't make ends meet. I am an inefficient and distracted employee, on a quit-or-be-fired path to the end of my career.

...

Pause to remember a time when you struggled with something that felt completely overwhelming.

...

One March night as Ben and I talk on the phone, my exhaustion is evident. He invites me to move into his apartment, no one is using it anyway.

We'll figure out the rest of it in a couple months, he says.

A few days later, I pick up my children from the soon-to-be-ex in the early morning hours before work. My son is not dressed. At the daycare I am rushing to get this child out of his pajamas and ready for his day. I am struggling to hold back tears.

Noticing bruises on my son—the faint blue shadow of a handprint—one of the caregivers reports child abuse. I am quickly cleared. When the time comes to return my children to my soon-to-be-ex I keep them with me. I have permission from the court. In Ben's apartment I sit in the darkness, watching for my estranged husband's car in the parking lot. I am grateful for the security building. I am afraid.

Years later I will get a call from his second wife telling me that she and my ex are getting a divorce. I will ask her: *How old are you?*

She will reply: *23.*

She is the same age I was the day my ex and I drew up the flimsy kitchen-table agreement to end our marriage.

I'm sorry, I say, standing near the kitchen window. *Thanks for letting us know.*

Us. Thanks for letting us know. Ben and I are married. He came back to Wisconsin from California. We followed his career to Iowa. He's adopted the kids and we've purchased our first home, a house on Cortina Avenue. Looking out the kitchen window I can see our back yard.

Ours is a story of three rings without storybook proposal. The first wedding ring a simple gold band purchased by me in a shopping mall jewelry store in the city where we first met, just days before our courthouse wedding in another state, when the romantic within me realized the no-ring thing wasn't really working for me.

The second ring, a secret purchase, a gift for Ben after our parish priest walked me through the hoops, hope and healing of annulment, then officiated the blessing of our marriage in the Catholic church.

The third ring, a ten diamond anniversary band, a surprise gift from my husband, the man God designed for me.

In the good years, marriage is fun and easy. In the years when I can do nothing but whine and complain the tall man stands by me. In the years when he is unhappy, I hold onto him.

God met us in the darkness and brought us into the light.

Do everything without complaining or arguing. Then you will be pure and without blame. You will be children of God without fault among sinful and evil people. Then you will shine among them like stars in the sky. – Philippians 2:14-15 NIRV

But the wisdom that is from above is first pure, then peaceable, gentle, willing to yield, full of mercy and good fruits, without partiality and without hypocrisy.
– James 3:17 NKJV

11

Love

I can't quite wrap my heart around it, but there was something so different about this man—the man who would become my husband—even on that first night and in the morning after, when our relationship could so easily have become a one-night stand.

Is it that we were naked and unashamed? [22]

Looking back over the weeks and months that followed, and the weekend together in California that preceded his first *I love you*, the memories unfold revealing words and actions and moments that felt so very right. The first is that night we met when he sits down at my table in the bar—that he actually sits down despite my dangerous and off-putting mood. I cherish that moment, the boldness he exhibited in sitting, that his actions caught me off guard. I never expected anyone to dare to sit down. That moment, the sitting down, the confident defiance, the acceptance of the challenge, his engaging in pursuit so boldly, is the moment my divorce-hardened heart cracked open. Without my knowledge or permission, my broken heart opened ever so slightly to the possibility of loving again.

> Without my knowledge or permission, my divorce-hardened heart opened ever so slightly to the possibility of loving again.

---

[22] The biblical story celebrating man and woman is found in Genesis 2:20-25.

. . .

Reflection:
Why do we, as couples, spend so much time
tracking the failures and the wounds
when there are greater moments of love
and grace and joy to celebrate?
How can we reverse the trend?

. . .

In the first 48 hours of our relationship there are several surprise moments.

Integrity amid the insanity: At a time when everyone in my circle of friends was falling into bed with strangers, he was the only man ever to sleep with me who asked about birth control beforehand, and expected me to provide proof before falling into bed again.

Rolodex card: He took my number then he actually called with plans—tickets to a play, a baseball game, lunches in restaurants, dinners at his apartment where he cooked for me. Despite my initial assumption that the Rolodex card indicated there were quite a few women in his life simultaneously, the amount of time we were spending together refuted that.

Even after sneaking into his home office and flipping through his Rolodex it still takes me an awfully long time to believe he is what he appears to be—a man with integrity.

. . .

Sneaking into his office and flipping through the
Rolodex is a betrayal of trust.
Reflection:
What prompts us to look?
What is the risk? What is the remedy?

. . .

Boundaries: My disco albums could not indiscriminately intermingle with his music—Warren Zevon, Mannheim Steamroller, Led Zepplin. If I intended to leave records at his apartment I'd need to write my name on the album covers.

He had other rules:
- ✓ last one out of the bed makes it
- ✓ if one of us cooks the other does dishes
- ✓ never run out of toilet paper.

In later years he and I added:
- ✓ sleep when you are tired
- ✓ eat when you are hungry.

After his death our daughter and I add one more:
- ✓ embrace joy whenever you find it.

. . .

Reflection:
How are boundaries helpful?
Who gets to decide?

. . .

Decades after we met—in our empty-nest season—there is a moment in our bedroom when he asks me what I find attractive about him. The question is a huge risk. He is being so very vulnerable. Without hesitating I respond: *The things that first attracted me are still here. I love that you are tall and intelligent, your sense of humor, the way you make me laugh, and sex.*

We laughed.

Today, as his widow, within me there is a need to remember deeply. Anxiety rises when I begin to believe that I will never hear his voice again. God is there. I remember a video he made of our grandson playing with rolls of architectural drawings on the floor of his office. His voice is there, on that video. His voice is recorded other places too.

When I long for his touch, remembering when he held me close and he smelled so good—he'd laugh at me, saying *it's just soap and water*.

Yes! Soap, shaving cream, scented deodorant—these things are still here in the bathroom cabinet—and the smell of his shaving cream brings me deep into the memory of being held in his arms.

Nearly a year before my husband's death, a close friend was doing research on divorce and had sent us surveys. My husband apparently found this interesting. He mentioned it while we were at dinner, celebrating our anniversary. We fully intended to share our responses with each other, yet never got around to it.

Today, as his widow, I find his responses soothing. Though he cannot be here to comfort me, his thoughts on marriage are here for me to read, an unexpected blessing, words revealed in God's perfect timing.

. . .

Pause to remember a time God provided
comfort for your pain.
Reflection:
How did you fully embrace it?
How did you refuse to accept it?

. . .

12

23 Again

My grief journals began with pages of poetry from the first two weeks, undated entries, random and dark:

> **Fortress**
> I smile and welcome
> the condolences
> the words of sympathy
> from this person before me
> unsolicited advice
> as though I am a moron without a clue
> or insight into death
> my soul dies back like withering grass
> at the edge of a desert
> that will not see rain
> life and light that once pushed outward
> to be free on the heavenly earth
> now detaches
> from the underside of my skin,
> pulling inward and away
> from the distaste
> the person hugging me
> is it only in darkness that I will be free?

Untitled

a cloud of pollen
I begin to sneeze
a week later
I am in bed
uncontrollable hacking
coughing
discomfort
fear that I will not breathe
fever rising
urine darkening
hours of sleep
and then
I give in
call in sick
my perfect record broken
as if attendance matters
no longer superwoman
I desperately need time off
to sleep
to rest
to sit with God in this mess
the unfamiliar patterns of grief
the alternation of clarity and confusion
spinning and darting
like lights on a police car
most moments
I cannot tell you
what day it is

Today

today my love
I awoke with the
most comforting
sensation
expecting you to be
on your side
of our bed
I am not even in our bed
but resting in the
guestroom
our bed is unmade
washed sheets
pillowcases
and quilt
in piles
awaiting hands
to weave the magic
that is making
a king size bed
today
this day
was the most
difficult day
perhaps because
of your nearness
as it started
perhaps because
it was a day
to do the widow work

I find myself holding my breath while the chaos of death swirls around me: the attorney and the will, the accountant and the taxes; the illusive balance between working and living; the pain of grieving and the promise of healing.

My journals record the details of my grief.

DAY 41

JOURNAL: I thought grief would be … Later.
Later in my life. It feels too soon.
I thought grief would be … Finite.
I am overwhelmed by the sense that I will feel this sad, this disconnected, this lost, forever.
I thought grief would be … Obvious.
Too often those who are claiming to love me most are oblivious to me, my needs, as though my pain is not obvious at all.

DAY 47

JOURNAL: Anxiety. Had a panic attack today—couldn't run, couldn't hide. Firmly put my hands palms-down on my dresser and shouted into the mirror: I will not be locked within cages of fear!

DAY 140

JOURNAL: I find that tears flow freely in the privacy of the shower and in the soft darkness of a weekly yoga class; that a cocktail after work to help me sleep is too easily dangerous and that chamomile tea is soothing, safe and warm; that the gritty shard of death becomes the pearl in the oyster, the irritant smoothed by time promises to emerge as something beautiful; that a caterpillar is cocooned in total darkness before her wings are ready for flight; that the sound of sirens is a signal for prayer; and that whatever I am feeling or thinking is not just ok, it is important—my mind and body are sending messages to me.

> ...
> *Pause to remember a time when you felt cocooned in darkness.*
> *Reflection:*
> *Did something beautiful emerge?*
> ...

Looking toward a future without my husband often triggers the pain of being 23 again. I can listen to the lies—the whispers of shame and hopelessness—choosing to stand on the bridge and contemplate my own death, as I did that summer.

Blog: Blackest Night

The railing is more substantial than expected. I'd driven across the bridge a thousand times, but this night for the first time I walk it. I am close enough to the railing to touch the smooth, round metal. The circumference is more than twice the distance measured palm to fingertip; my two hands together look too small to fully grasp it.

Walking the 4½ miles from a friend's spare bedroom in Camino Park to the bridge on South Hastings Way did not alleviate my desperation. Step followed step. Seconds gathered into minutes. An hour passed without memory as though a dense fog had swallowed up the visual and visceral cues that life exists.

I experience myself without dimension from somewhere deep within, a heartbeat slows and grows loud, pulses a primal accompaniment, intensifying my need for escape.

The air is cool. Its breeze delivers a hint of fall. The river below is still and soundless, lifeless and black. Day has turned to evening.

The night is swallowing the sun.

My hands move toward the railing. Headlamps on a passing car illuminate a large black spider, the builder of an intricate web anchored to the smooth, round metal. I am startled and fearful, eyes alert and intent on this unexpected adversary, hands now motionless in midair, heart and soul moving as though in meditation: behold the delicate web.

The bridge had been my destination, the inky black river my intended tomb.

Behold the delicate web: intricate and anchored, woven and unwavering.

Blackest night cannot devour the sun.[23]

When you beg the Lord for help, he will answer, "Here I am!" – Isaiah 5:9 CEV

I walked off the bridge that night, in the summer of 1985, and walked another couple of miles to Ben's apartment. For decades he was the only person who knew the depth of my pain.

Now in the wake of his death I need not stand alone. Walking off the bridge today, choosing to make my way to the sweet earth of the riverbank, I can wade back into community and rejoin the river of life—trusting that God, Immanuel, is with us.

---

[23] *A brutal battle for custody in the midst of shattered dreams. The isolation of divorce. Economic poverty.* – endnote, *Blackest Night*.

An angel of the Lord appeared to him in a dream and said, "Joseph son of David, do not be afraid to take Mary home as your wife, because what is conceived in her is from the Holy Spirit. [21] She will give birth to a son, and you are to give him the name Jesus, because he will save his people from their sins."

[22] All this took place to fulfill what the Lord had said through the prophet: [23] "The virgin will conceive and give birth to a son, and they will call him Immanuel" (which means "God with us").

– Matthew 1:20-23

13

Performance Theater

In my husband's inbox there is an email. It is from our daughter inviting him to build sets for *The Wizard of Oz*. She auditioned—terribly to hear her tell it.

It's been years since she appeared on stage as the fairy godmother in *Cinderella*. It was for Cinderella's fairy godmother that Dad first pitched in to build sets.

He died the next morning, the day after her email arrived. On the day he died time stopped for both our children.

Opening night of *The Wizard of Oz* is joyful and tearful as she and I remember Dad, the man who never missed a performance. Presence is a beautiful and lasting gift.

As summer turns to fall *Into The Woods* embraces her Florinda, and we find comfort in celebrating life alongside the people we love most. We are remembering the past and making way for the future, trusting that God is with us every step of the way.

> *No, I will not abandon you as orphans—I will come to you. [19] Soon the world will no longer see me, but you will see me. Since I live, you also will live. [20] When I am raised to life again, you will know that I am in my Father, and you are in me, and I am in you.*
>
> *— John 14:18-21* NLT

. . .

Reflection:
How are you trusting God?
How are you making way for the future?

. . .

14

Surrender

My task now is to write the final chapter, the story of reliance on God, the story unfolding in my widowhood.

When the living room was filled with emergency responders and the police sergeant asked me if there were anyone I needed to call five names came to mind. Of these first five, three were women, trained therapists and true friends. Each one helped me grieve, invited me to breathe, cared for me.

It wasn't enough.

These talented and faithful women and the two strong, intelligent men—also in the first five names that came to mind—could not withstand the full weight of this painful, crushing grief.

Only God could do that.

What I coming to realize is that the strong and mighty hands of God are also warm and lush and gentle, that I am cradled, precious, safe. There is no need to dry my tears, no need to muffle the awful sound of my keening, or hide the depth of my hopelessness. God is here to comfort me, every moment, day or night. He is in every breath my body takes.

God sent five strong people to surround me in the first moment, people who were the hands and feet and heart of Christ. Others came too, walking beside me, because I will cry again tomorrow—tears of grief and tears of joy.

Rejoice in the Lord always; again I will say, rejoice. ⁵ Let your reasonableness be known to everyone. The Lord is at hand; ⁶ do not be anxious about anything, but in everything by prayer and supplication with thanksgiving let your requests be made known to God. ⁷ And the peace of God, which surpasses all understanding, will guard your hearts and your minds in Christ Jesus. – Philippians 4:4-7 ESV

In my widowhood, there is regret I carry—that in this life I did not take my pain, frustration, anger and sadness to God before burdening my husband.

When my husband was living I often went to him first. If I had this life to do over again, I'd give to God my problems at work, or that frustrating person, or meeting, or phone call. I'd face my neediness, then pray, asking God for wisdom, resilience and comfort.

I'd not spend time with my husband rehashing the negativity of this world. Instead, I'd fully embrace life in a way that whenever I walked in the door and called out, *Honey, I'm home,* my heart would be free to engage my husband with love and joy and laughter.

. . .

Reflection:
How will you engage your beloved one?
What will you ask of God?

. . .

Resources

Blog: My Eulogy

Renee wanted us to remember the 5th grader, the girl deeply wounded and passionately driven. A young woman who refused to accept the idea, *I can't. I can't because I'm a girl.* A habitual speeder, a magnet for traffic citations. A woman who had trouble relinquishing the steering wheel to God. A woman for whom wisdom and a quiet spirit were an uphill battle.

A woman who left this world having it all. Having changed lives, a handful of lives, the lives and hearts God asked her to touch. Having loved and served God; loved and cherished her husband, the man God designed to be her closest friend; loved and mentored and comforted her children, while hoping and praying she was teaching her children to love. Having lived with authenticity, stretched herself, challenged us to something greater, helped us to stretch and reach. Having embraced grief and joy on her earthly journey, living her life in a way that left no doubt God is with us.

I have told you this so that my joy may be in you and that your joy may be complete. My command is this: Love each other as I have loved you. Greater love has no one than this: to lay down one's life for one's friends. – John 15:11-13

My Life Verse, Words to Guide Me

But what happens when we live God's way? He brings gifts into our lives, much the same way that fruit appears in an orchard—things like affection for others, exuberance about life, serenity. We develop a willingness to stick with things, a sense of compassion in the heart, and a conviction that a basic holiness permeates things and people. We find ourselves involved in loyal commitments, not needing to force our way in life, able to marshal and direct our energies wisely. – Galatians 5:22-23 MSG

But the fruit of the Spirit is love, joy, peace, patience, kindness, goodness, faithfulness, gentleness, self-control; against such things there is no law.
– Galatians 5:22-23 NASB

Scriptures from our Celebration of Life

Listen to my words, LORD, consider my lament. ² Hear my cry for help, my King and my God, for to you I pray.³ **In the morning, LORD, you hear my voice; in the morning I lay my requests before you and wait expectantly.** *⁴ For you are not a God who is pleased with wickedness; with you, evil people are not welcome. ⁵ The arrogant cannot stand in your presence. You hate all who do wrong; ⁶ you destroy those who tell lies. The bloodthirsty and deceitful you, LORD, detest.⁷ But I, by your great love, can come into your house; in reverence I bow down toward your holy temple.* – Psalm 5:1-7 *emphasis added*

I will give thanks to you, LORD, with all my heart; I will tell of all your wonderful deeds.² I will be glad and rejoice in you; I will sing the praises of your name, O Most High. ³ My enemies turn back; they stumble and perish before you. ⁴ For you have upheld my right and my cause, sitting enthroned as the righteous judge. ⁵ You have rebuked the nations and destroyed the wicked; you have blotted out their name for ever and ever.⁶ Endless ruin has overtaken my enemies, you have uprooted their cities; even the memory of them has perished ...

¹³ Relent, LORD! How long will it be? Have compassion on your servants.¹⁴ **Satisfy us in the morning with your unfailing love, that we may sing for joy and be glad all our days.** *¹⁵ Make us glad for as many days as you have afflicted us, for as many years as we have seen trouble. ¹⁶ May your deeds be shown*

to your servants, your splendor to their children.
¹⁷ May the favor of the Lord our God rest on us; establish the work of our hands for us—yes, establish the work of our hands.

– Psalm 90:1-6, 13-17 *emphasis added*

On his arrival, Jesus found that Lazarus had already been in the tomb for four days. ¹⁸ Now Bethany was less than two miles from Jerusalem, ¹⁹ and many Jews had come to Martha and Mary to comfort them in the loss of their brother. ²⁰ When Martha heard that Jesus was coming, she went out to meet him, but Mary stayed at home.

²¹ "Lord," Martha said to Jesus, "if you had been here, my brother would not have died. ²² But I know that even now God will give you whatever you ask."

²³ Jesus said to her, "Your brother will rise again."

²⁴ Martha answered, "I know he will rise again in the resurrection at the last day."

²⁵ Jesus said to her, "I am the resurrection and the life. The one who believes in me will live, even though they die; ²⁶ and whoever lives by believing in me will never die. Do you believe this?"

²⁷ **"Yes, Lord,"** *she replied,* **"I believe that you are the Messiah, the Son of God, who is to come into the world."**

²⁸ After she had said this, she went back and called her sister Mary aside. "The Teacher is here," she said, "and is asking for you." ²⁹ When Mary heard this, she got up quickly and went to him. ³⁰ Now Jesus had not yet entered the village, but was still at the place where

Martha had met him. ³¹ When the Jews who had been with Mary in the house, comforting her, noticed how quickly she got up and went out, they followed her, supposing she was going to the tomb to mourn there.

³² When Mary reached the place where Jesus was and saw him, she fell at his feet and said, "Lord, if you had been here, my brother would not have died."

³³ When Jesus saw her weeping, and the Jews who had come along with her also weeping, he was deeply moved in spirit and troubled. ³⁴ "Where have you laid him?" he asked.

"Come and see, Lord," they replied.

³⁵ Jesus wept.

³⁶ Then the Jews said, "See how he loved him!"

³⁷ But some of them said, "Could not he who opened the eyes of the blind man have kept this man from dying?"

³⁸ Jesus, once more deeply moved, came to the tomb. It was a cave with a stone laid across the entrance. ³⁹ "Take away the stone," he said.

"But, Lord," said Martha, the sister of the dead man, "by this time there is a bad odor, for he has been there four days."

⁴⁰ Then Jesus said, "Did I not tell you that if you believe, you will see the glory of God?"

⁴¹ So they took away the stone. Then Jesus looked up and said, "Father, I thank you that you have heard me. ⁴² I knew that you always hear me, but I said this for the benefit of the people standing here, that they may believe that you sent me."

⁴³ When he had said this, Jesus called in a loud voice, "Lazarus, come out!" ⁴⁴ The dead man came out, his hands and feet wrapped with strips of linen, and a cloth around his face.

Jesus said to them, "Take off the grave clothes and let him go." – John 11:17-44 *emphasis added*

Scriptures included in *Widowspeak*

2 Samuel 12:20-23 NASB	pg 13
John 10:10 NASB	13
Zephaniah 3:17 NKJV	13
John 14:2-4 ESV	18
Psalm 139:16 VOICE	21
Psalm 147:3	27
Psalm 34:18	31
2 Timothy 2:20-22 CEV	32
1 Peter 3:1-6	33-34
Acts 2:42-47	35
Matthew 6:25-34	41
John 11:1-16 NLT	47-48
John 12:7-8	48
Hebrews 4:15-16 ESV	51
John 12:1-8	54
Philippians 2:14-15 NIRV	69
James 3:17 NKJV	69
Isaiah 5:9 CEV	80
Matthew 1:20-23	81
John 14:18-21 NLT	83
Philippians 4:4-7 ESV	86
John 15:11-13	89
Galatians 5:22-23 MSG	90
Galatians 5:22-23 NASB	90
Psalm 5:1-7	91
Psalm 90:1-6, 13-17	91-92
John 11:17-44	92-94
Isaiah 40:31	98

CEV © copyright American Bible Society
ESV © copyright Crossway
MSG © copyright NavPress Publishing Group
NASB © copyright The Lockman Foundation
NIRV © copyright Biblica Inc
NKJV © copyright Thomas Nelson
VOICE © copyright Ecclesia Bible Study

Unless otherwise indicated, scripture used is
NLT © copyright Tyndale House Foundation

Notes

[1] Guilt is *I did something*, Shame is *I am something* – Andrea M. Polnaszek, LCSW, author of *The Elijah Project*, identifying our feelings and learning to express our emotions in a God honoring way, andreapolnaszek.com.

[2] The biblical story of Jesus raising Lazarus from the dead is in John 11:1-44.

[3] *I am … a flawed, human and fragile encourager* is from my blog, the self-descriptive words I first embraced in 2009.

[4] *The Ingenious Nobleman Sir Quixote of La Mancha* is a Spanish novel by Miguel de Cervantes Saavedra. See also, the movie *Man of La Mancha* (1972) starring Peter O'Toole, Sophia Loren and James Coco.

[5] *Heartbeat* was written as an assignment from the Trust Yourself (#Trust30) Writing Challenge an online initiative of Seth Godin and The Domino Project, including quotes from Ralph Waldo Emerson.

[6] Source: *A Widow's Guide to Healing: Gentle Support and Advice for the First 5 Years* by Kristin Meekhof, LMSW and James Windell, MA.

[7] The Global Leadership Summit simulcast, willowcreek.com.

[8] The biblical story of Elijah is in 1 Kings 16-19, 21-22 and 2 Kings 1-2.

[9] Red Tent Living is an invitation. Amidst all of the impossible, confusing, and shaming ideas of what femininity is in our culture today, we find respite and meaning in gathering together, redtentliving.com.

[10] *Processing Through Grief: Guided Exercises to Understand Your Emotions and Recover From Loss* by Stephanie Jose, LMHC, LCAT. Foreword by Cécile Rêve, LMHC.

[11] *The 7 Habits of Highly Effective People: Powerful Lessons in Personal Change* and *The 8th Habit: From Effectiveness to Greatness,* Stephen R. Covey, author.

[12] *My Eulogy* published in my blog in March 2012, is included in *Resources*.

[13] Scrabble® is a game my paternal grandmother played with me and my cousins, one I played often with my husband, and a joy I hope to one day share with our grandchildren.

[14] In the teachings of Dan B. Allender, PhD, my heart discovered great healing. Dan Allender and Tremper Longman's GOD LOVES SEX is especially delightful and the only book I ever purchased that my husband voluntarily picked up from the dining room table then finished reading before I did!

[15] *Processing Through Grief*, Ibid.

[16] My journals contain several styles of cursive handwriting reflecting the scattered state of my mind and heart.

[17] Adapted from *Prayer in Time of Bereavement*, catholic.org.

[18] *Wounded Heart: Hope for Adult Victims of Childhood Sexual Abuse* by Dan B. Allender, PhD. Foreword by Larry Crabb, PhD.

[19] *The Elijah Project* series by Andrea M. Polnaszek, LCSW.

[20] Written in 2008 *Blue Flannel LAX* reveals my struggle, the chaos of divorce, economic poverty, single motherhood, promiscuity, public shame and private fear—the broken person I was when God brought Ben to me.

[21] *Pretty Woman* (1990) starring Richard Geer and Julia Roberts.

[22] The biblical story celebrating man and woman is found in Genesis 2:20-25.

[23] *A brutal battle for custody in the midst of shattered dreams. The isolation of divorce. Economic poverty.* – endnote, *Blackest Night*.

About the Author

Renee J. Wurzer

In her first book, *Widowspeak*, Renee Wurzer moves from proofreading to publishing, from editing to writing, from behind the curtain to center stage.

A recent widow, her delight here on earth is her legacy family, especially the grandchildren. She considers herself an encourager and writes daily, publishing her work online as she engages the journey from grief to joy.

Renew Collaborative

A deep appreciation for the written word, a passion for well-told stories and her affection for perfection, inspire Renee Wurzer to support and encourage writers seeking to self-publish books and other creative works. Join her in this newest venture, Renew Collaborative.

website: renewcollaborative.com
email: renew@bloomer.net
facebook: @renewcollaborative
twitter: @Renee9330083
blog: whisperedhopes.blogspot.com

The name *Renew Collaborative* was inspired by the
Isaiah 40:31 mixed-media painting created by Destiny Jackson

but those who hope in the Lord
will renew their strength.
They will soar on wings like eagles;
they will run and not grow weary,
they will walk and not be faint.

CPSIA information can be obtained
at www.ICGtesting.com
Printed in the USA
LVHW021558120819
627349LV00012B/1120/P